ISBN 978-1-331-50118-3
PIBN 10198620

# 1 MONTH OF
# FREE
# READING

## at

## www.ForgottenBooks.com

By purchasing this book you are eligible for one month membership to ForgottenBooks.com, giving you unlimited access to our entire collection of over 1,000,000 titles via our web site and mobile apps.

To claim your free month visit:
www.forgottenbooks.com/free198620

S. HRG. 103–78

# NOMINATION OF ROBERT M. SUSSMAN

4. P 96/10: S. HRG. 103-78

onination of Robert M. Sussman, S....

# HEARING

### BEFORE THE

# COMMITTEE ON
# ENVIRONMENT AND PUBLIC WORKS
# UNITED STATES SENATE

## ONE HUNDRED THIRD CONGRESS

### FIRST SESSION

ON

THE NOMINATION OF ROBERT M. SUSSMAN, TO BE DEPUTY
ADMINISTRATOR, ENVIRONMENTAL PROTECTION AGENCY

APRIL 28, 1993

Printed for the use of the Committee on Environment and Public Works

U.S. GOVERNMENT PRINTING OFFICE
WASHINGTON : 1993

87-639

# NOMINATION OF ROBERT M. SUSSMAN

4. P 96/10: S. HRG. 103-78

onination of Robert M. Sussman, S....

# HEARING

BEFORE THE

## COMMITTEE ON
## ENVIRONMENT AND PUBLIC WORKS
## UNITED STATES SENATE

ONE HUNDRED THIRD CONGRESS

FIRST SESSION

ON

THE NOMINATION OF ROBERT M. SUSSMAN, TO BE DEPUTY
ADMINISTRATOR, ENVIRONMENTAL PROTECTION AGENCY

APRIL 28, 1993

Printed for the use of the Committee on Environment and Public Works

U.S. GOVERNMENT PRINTING OFFICE
WASHINGTON · 1993

87–839

## COMMITTEE ON ENVIRONMENT AND PUBLIC WORKS

MAX BAUCUS, Montana, *Chairman*

DANIEL PATRICK MOYNIHAN, New York
GEORGE J. MITCHELL, Maine
FRANK R. LAUTENBERG, New Jersey
HARRY REID, Nevada
BOB GRAHAM, Florida
JOSEPH I. LIEBERMAN, Connecticut
HOWARD M. METZENBAUM, Ohio
HARRIS WOFFORD, Pennsylvania
BARBARA BOXER, California

JOHN H. CHAFEE, Rhode Island
ALAN K. SIMPSON, Wyoming
DAVE DURENBERGER, Minnesota
JOHN W. WARNER, Virginia
ROBERT SMITH, New Hampshire
LAUCH FAIRCLOTH, North Carolina
DIRK KEMPTHORNE, Idaho

PETER L. SCHER, *Staff Director*
STEVEN J. SHIMBERG, *Minority Staff Director and Chief Counsel*

(II)

# C O N T E N T S

## OPENING STATEMENTS

|  | Page |
|---|---|
| Baucus, Hon. Max, U.S. Senator from the State of Montana | 1 |
| Chafee, Hon. John H., U.S. Senator from the State of Rhode Island | 10 |
| Kempthorne, Hon. Dirk, U.S. Senator from the State of Idaho | 3 |

## WITNESS

| | |
|---|---|
| Sussman, Robert M., nominated to be Deputy Administrator, Environmental Protection Agency | 5 |
| Prepared statement | 21 |
| Responses to a committee questionnaire | 27 |

(III)

# NOMINATION OF ROBERT M. SUSSMAN

---

## WEDNESDAY, APRIL 28, 1993

U.S. SENATE,
COMMITTEE ON ENVIRONMENT AND PUBLIC WORKS,
*Washington, DC.*

The committee met, pursuant to notice, at 9:35 a.m. in room 406, Dirksen Senate Office Building, Hon. Max Baucus (chairman of the committee) presiding.

Present: Senators Baucus, Kempthorne, Chafee, and Faircloth.

## OPENING STATEMENT OF HON. MAX BAUCUS, U.S. SENATOR FROM THE STATE OF MONTANA

Senator BAUCUS. The hearing will come to order.

Good morning. The Committee on Environment and Public Works today meets to consider the nomination of Robert Sussman to be Deputy Administrator of the Environmental Protection Agency.

I first want to welcome you to the hearing, Mr. Sussman.

At this point I also think it would be appropriate if you could introduce your family to everyone here. I'm sure it's a big honor for them, as it is for you to have them here, so could you please introduce your family to the committee?

Mr. SUSSMAN. I would be happy to. It is a special pleasure to have them here today.

First I would like to introduce my mother, Gertrude Sussman, a very important person in my life—in fact, all three are; my sister, Frances Sussman, and my wife, Judith.

We have a two-and-a-half-year-old son who——

Senator BAUCUS. So there is another man in your family.

Mr. SUSSMAN. Absolutely, a very impressive one. He is here in spirit today, but we thought the better part of valor would be not to have him here in person. [Laughter.]

Senator BAUCUS. Thank you very much, Mr. Sussman.

The Deputy Administrator, as you know, assists the Administrator—a very able Administrator in Carol Browner—in supervising and directing programs and activities of the Environmental Protection Agency, which I hope is about to be the new Department of Environment.

If Mr. Sussman is confirmed, he will help implement and enforce the Nation's environmental laws and supervise nearly 18,000 employees, and manage almost $7 billion.

As daunting a task as that seems, your job entails much more than that. The public expects you to help break the gridlock that has blocked many of the solutions to our Nation's environmental problems. As Deputy Administrator, your job is to help replace this gridlock with cooperation so we can formulate policies that will lead our Nation into the 21st century as global environmental leaders.

This should be very challenging and very exciting. Frankly, I think it calls for a new way of thinking about our Nation and our people, our natural resources, and also about our environment. It means being bold, bolder than we have in many cases been in the past; it means reaching out for new ideas, much more creative than we have been; finding out what's broken and fixing it; and dispelling old myths, like the myth that we must necessarily choose between a clean environment and a strong economy.

That dangerous myth drives Americans apart. The fact is, a clean environment and a strong economy are really two sides of the same coin. They are both based on simple, fundamental ideas: planning ahead; investing in the future, rather than squandering resources; and building a better life together for our children.

Ultimately we will have both good jobs and a clean environment or we will have neither. They go hand-in-hand.

Mr. Sussman, you and the Administrator have enormous potential to dispel this old myth and to break the gridlock by replacing confrontation with cooperation and get on with the task of better protecting our Nation's environment and natural resources.

You obviously have experience in developing this solution. You have worked hard in developing environmental regulations through negotiation with environmental organizations, with the EPA, and with industry, and you will need to build on this experience to find progressive and pragmatic solutions to environmental problems through cooperation rather than through confrontation.

We have a number of major environmental statutes that must be reauthorized, including Superfund, Safe Drinking Water Act, Clean Water Act, and our solid hazardous waste laws. As we proceed with these reauthorizations we must reach out to the States and work much more cooperatively with them than we have in the past; we must reach out to the cities and all affected parties in an effort to assess how well our environmental laws are working and how they can be improved.

We must explore ways to integrate our laws better. For example, does it still make sense to address each environmental law independently?

We must look for ways to cut the administrative red tape and the bureaucratic hoops in our laws and regulations so we can protect the environment more directly and efficiently, and we must continue to build a solid foundation through better science and research and development as a basis for our decisions. We will then have a solid basis to reauthorize our environmental statutes.

Obviously, the key is to work together. If we are to succeed, we must cooperate and look for progressive, fair, and responsible solutions to our problems. If we do, there is no question in my mind that we will succeed. The Clinton Administration has shown that it intends to work with the Congress on policies to ensure that we will be global leaders in the 21st century. I welcome this opportunity, and I am certain that as Deputy Administrator of EPA you, too, will work with the Congress to provide a better environment for every American.

I wish you very well, and thank you for appearing before us today. I look forward to working very closely with you.

I would now like to turn to a very able Senator on this committee and a very aggressive new member on this committee, from a State adjoining mine to the west of Montana, Senator Kempthorne.

## OPENING STATEMENT OF HON. DIRK KEMPTHORNE, U.S. SENATOR FROM THE STATE OF IDAHO

Senator KEMPTHORNE. Thank you, Mr. Chairman.

Mr. Chairman, I have formal comments for an opening statement that I would just ask be included in the record.

Senator BAUCUS. Without objection.

Senator KEMPTHORNE. And to Mr. Sussman I would say congratulations on the nomination. I appreciated your courtesy in coming by and I enjoyed our visit. The members of your family must be proud.

I would just make note and state publicly that as you referenced the fact that you have a two-and-a-half-year-old son, while you meet the challenges of this new position, make sure that you find time for that young family. That is also critically important.

I look forward to your comments and I have some questions at the appropriate time.

Mr. Chairman, thank you.

[Senator Kempthorne's statement follows:]

OPENING STATEMENT OF HON. DIRK KEMPTHORNE, U.S. SENATOR FROM THE STATE OF
                          IDAHO

Mr. Chairman, thank you; and Mr. Sussman, I appreciate your appearance
before the Committee today to advise us of your views and your anticipated
approach to the responsibilities that will be yours, if confirmed. I hope
this will be the first of many appearances and that your working relationship
with this' Committee and its members will always be one of candor, cooperation,
and forward-thinking.

Environmental policy and its enforcement has matured, and I believe now
is a good time to evaluate how far we have come in this country, where we want
to go further, and how best that is to be accomplished. As Deputy
Administrator to Carol Browner, you will be in a position to effect changes at
the Environmental Protection Agency. Those are long overdue; and while much
of your agenda at the Agency will be the one set by the Administrator, and by
White House priorities, I hope that you alert us today to some of the
priorities that you will council Carol Browner to address early.

The Environmental Protection Agency has been notorious for its heavy
handed approach to states, and in particular to local government. It is
perhaps an example of top-down government, with not as much attention to
concerns, issues, and ideas expressed coming back in the other direction.

The effects of EPA decisions, rule-makings, and enforcement actions are
intensely local. The recent enactment of the Clean Air Act Amendments has
augmented the EPA's already substantial ability to determine the economic
vitality of local communities. Through its rule-making authority, EPA has more
often than not favored an expansive and intrusive regulatory approach,
insensitive to the practical and predictable consequences of the regulatory
burden it imposes. I have seen EPA's approach to enforcement swallow up the
already limited budgets of local communities, demanding technical compliance
with rules that will achieve no additional real benefit in water quality for
the local community. In the process, funds are diverted from more genuine and
pressing concerns in that community.

I am not suggesting that EPA should ignore real compliance problems at
the local level. What I am saying is that EPA needs to do a far better job
than it has to date in establishing a partnership with state and local
governments and private businesses and individuals for the protection of our
environment. It needs to favor the least burdensome regulatory approach; it
needs to allow for greater autonomy and flexibility; it especially needs to
streamline the demands it makes for paperwork and data collection, and take
into better account the practical experience that individuals, businesses, and
local communities have in attempting to live under and comply with the
nation's environmental laws and the regulations EPA has promulgated to
implement them.

I hope that during your watch at the EPA, you will be able to move the
Agency in this, more responsive, direction. I hope that you will be in the
forefront of the movement to recognize that economic growth and environmental
protection are not incompatible. Both of these are essential elements of the
stewardship that we hold, and EPA's vision should be to harness rather than
tamp out the energy, creativity, and vitality necessary to fulfill that
stewardship.

I look forward to hearing from you, Mr. Sussman.

Senator BAUCUS. Thank you, Senator.

Mr. Sussman, why don't you p        with your statement? Your prepared remarks will be includedbcæedhe record, and at this point you can proceed in any way that you wish.

## STATEMENT OF ROBERT M. SUSSMAN, NOMINATED TO BE DEPUTY ADMINISTRATOR, ENVIRONMENTAL PROTECTION AGENCY

Mr. SUSSMAN. Thank you very much, Senator Baucus.

On behalf of myself and Administrator Browner, I want to thank the committee for the opportunity to appear at this hearing, and particularly thank the committee for the opportunity to meet informally as I have with many members and their staffs over the last two weeks. These meetings provided me with a very valuable understanding of the agenda of the committee and will help me immensely in performing my responsibilities if I am confirmed.

I am very honored that the President and the Administrator have asked me to serve as the EPA Deputy Administrator. As Senator Baucus observed, this is a challenging and demanding job, but also one that potentially offers very great rewards. This Administration is committed to a new vision of environmental protection that will change the relationship between our citizens and the world around us. As you indicated, Senator Baucus, economic growth and strong environmental safeguards are not incompatible; in fact, they are mutually reinforcing. This is a vision that I share and am deeply committed to, and if I am confirmed, I will do all I can to help the Administrator make it a reality.

I wanted to begin by sharing a few observations with the committee about my background and experience.

I was born in New York City shortly after the end of World War II. I consider myself part of the "baby boomer" generation. Although I haven't lived in New York for 20 years, I still consider it my home.

I went to college and law school in the late 1960's and early 1970's, and I believe that I was very much shaped by the idealism of that turbulent and difficult, but in many ways hopeful, period in our history. I became a practicing lawyer in Washington in 1974. My practice has primarily involved health, safety, and environmental issues, although I have devoted considerable time to pro bono work.

In the course of my practice I have worked extensively with environmental groups, EPA, and other agencies. I have developed great respect for the environmental community, the leadership and determination of which have helped to forge many of the successful environmental programs that are in place today. I have also developed great respect for EPA's career staff, whose extraordinary professionalism, expertise, and capacity for hard work have sustained the agency during the difficult periods in its history, and also made possible the many positive accomplishments that the agency has achieved.

Based on my experience over the last 20 years, I feel I have developed valuable skills that could help EPA meet the challenges that it faces. They include not only extensive knowledge of environmental science and policy, but more importantly, patience, a willingness to listen to the concerns of EPA's many stakeholders, and a strong commitment to consensus-building. I take considerable pride in the key role I played in negotiated rulemaking when I was in private practice. I hope to use this experience to help the Administrator fulfill her goal of building new partnerships among EPA, State and local governments, industry, and the environmental community.

I want to stress another important point. Although consensus and dialog are essential regulatory tools, EPA has the ultimate responsibility to set environmental goals for our Nation and to decide how those goals should be met. These functions require strong and farsighted leadership by the agency. EPA should certainly listen to the views of its stakeholders, but in the end the agency has an obligation to make clear p      choices and to communicate those choices to the regulated community in a manner which is timely and understandable. Standards and regulations implementing those policies should then be enforced fairly but vigorously.

In my work with industry I have observed first-hand the value of ambitious technology-forcing standards which challenge our companies to make the investments we need for long-term environmental improvement and economic growth. I am convinced that if EPA exercises strong leadership, American industry will cooperate with the agency and use its considerable talents to meet and surpass EPA's environmental goals without any loss of competitiveness.

As we look down the road, EPA's leadership role will be tested as we tackle the many unfinished portions of our environmental agenda. The Administrator has identified several ambitious goals for the agency, and if I am confirmed, it will be my role to help her achieve them. I would like to highlight some of those goals briefly in order to illustrate the areas where I hope to make a contribution to the agency if I am confirmed.

First, pollution prevention should be a cornerstone of all of EPA's programs so that our industries have every incentive to use waste minimization and new manufacturing processes to prevent the creation of pollution at the source. Pollution prevention can lessen our reliance on end-of-pipe controls, which are often ineffective. It can also help stimulate the technological innovation that we need for economic growth.

Second, ecosystem protection should become a goal of EPA's programs, equal in importance to the protection of human health. This means a new sensitivity to ecological concerns in EPA's decision-making and a new emphasis on geographical initiatives and cross-media programs.

Third, EPA should continue to improve the science base it uses for decisionmaking. This involves not only strengthening the quality of the data on which EPA relies, but more importantly, assuring that the agency seeks the most knowledgeable experts inside and outside the agency when it tackles complex and important scientific issues.

Fourth, EPA should build new partnerships with State and local governments that strengthen our environmental structure, streamline decisionmaking, and use Federal resources to support State programs better.

Finally, environmental justice should become a guiding principle for decisionmaking at EPA. Minority and low income communities should not be subjected disproportionately to environmental hazards, and they should be fully included in the decisionmaking process at EPA and at the State and local levels.

As the committee knows, the Administrator is committed to tackling not just these, but other critical environmental issues facing our Nation. If I am confirmed, it will be an honor to assist her in any way I can. I will also make every effort to build a productive and cooperative relationship with the Congress generally, and with this committee in particular.

Again, it is a great pleasure to be here today, and I will be very pleased to answer your questions.

Senator BAUCUS. Thank you very much, Mr. Sussman.

I have a couple of obligatory questions that I want to ask first.

Number one, are you willing, at the request of any duly-constituted committee of the Congress, to appear in front of it as a witness?

Mr. SUSSMAN. Yes, I am, Mr. Chairman.

Senator BAUCUS. Do you know of any matters which you may or may not have thus far disclosed which might place you in any conflict of interest if you are confirmed in this position?

Mr. SUSSMAN. I believe all potential conflicts of interest have been disclosed to the committee and to the EPA Ethics Officer.

Senator BAUCUS. You have a fairly exhaustive recusal policy, as in your statement to the committee you outline that you will recuse yourself permanently in several instances, and in another portion of your statement you listed some clients that you have recused yourself from.

My question is, would the scope of your recusal prevent you from carrying out your duties? I wonder if you could expand on that answer that you're going to give a little bit, please.

Mr. SUSSMAN. OK, I would be happy to.

Let me first indicate that I take this recusal statement very seriously. We spent a lot of time working with the EPA Ethics Officer and the Office of Government Ethics to make sure that we identified all the issues and nailed them down.

I am going to honor this statement very rigorously if I am confirmed, and I am confident that the statement will avoid all actual or potential conflicts of interest.

At the same time, Mr. Chairman, I feel that notwithstanding the statement, I will be free to play a broad and effective role in managing the agency. While I was an active practicing lawyer, I did have a number of clients. My work was basically limited to certain narrow areas of the agency's activities. These principally comprised rulemakings, enforcement actions, and judicial review proceedings under the Toxic Substances Control Act. I'm going to stay far away from all of the activities in which I was involved, but I want to make sure the committee understands that there were large categories of agency activities in which I did not participate as a private attorney. I was not involved as a private practitioner in the Superfund program, the RCRA program, the Clean Water program, and I was only minimally involved in the Air program. Therefore I believe I am not disabled in any way from addressing the issues presented by those programs or the general policy and management issues that fall within the purview of the Deputy Administrator.

Senator BAUCUS. What about FIFRA and TSCA, again? Those two areas?

Mr. SUSSMAN. TSCA is an area where I will need to tread very carefully. I did do a great deal of work under TSCA. That was my main area of concentration. There are a number of pending proceedings that I will be recused from, although as the TSCA program evolves and new issues come up, I should be able to address them.

I don't think that the FIFRA program presents any significant concern. There was one set of proceedings involving tributyl–10 paints that I handled when I was in private practice, but that was a proceeding of fairly limited scope. Other than that I have not been involved in the FIFRA program, so I think I should have fairly broad room to maneuver there.

Senator BAUCUS. Why do you want this job? What do you hope to accomplish? What mark do you want to leave?

Mr. SUSSMAN. Well, those are good questions and I've had to think a lot about them. Let me say at the outset that while this may sound somewhat maudlin, public service is very important to me and always has been. I am very excited that I have the opportunity to serve, to make a difference in this Administration. I am a strong supporter of the President and his program. I believe his environmental program is very exciting.

The environment has always had special meaning for me and for my family. I think that EPA is an agency that could be a great force for good in our society. I would like to be able to make a difference in any way I can.

So I am excited by the opportunity and hopeful that my talents can be used to help the agency make this country a better place.

Senator BAUCUS. Thank you. I'll have more questions, but thank you very much.

Senator Kempthorne.

Senator KEMPTHORNE. Thank you, Mr. Chairman.

Mr. Sussman, how would you describe the relationship between local units of government and the EPA, and the business community and its relationship with EPA?

Mr. SUSSMAN. Let me start with the State and local governments and make the following observation.

Many of our principal environmental statues have been in place for several years. As they have matured, day-to-day implementation responsibility has increasingly been transferred to the States. Now, after 15 or 20 years, we find that the States are on the front lines under RCRA, the Clean Water Act, the Clean Air Act.

EPA needs to have a constructive partnership with those States. It needs to help them do their job and not interfere with that. In my mind, this means streamlining oversight wherever possible; encouraging timely action by States; providing States with constructive technical and policy assistance when they need it; and not getting in the way when the States are capable of doing the job themselves.

EPA can improve in that area, as the Administrator has indicated. I hope to work with her on that.

As the committee well knows, the States are strapped for resources. In many cases they lack the full capability to discharge the responsibilities that the Federal Government has placed on them. EPA needs to do what it can to strengthen State capacity. I would note that the President's 1994 budget includes a proposal to create a Drinking Water State Revolving Fund which would respond to many of the concerns that have been expressed by the States about the burdens placed on them under the Safe Drinking Water Act. I think that's a constructive proposal.

Senator KEMPTHORNE. On that point, Mr. Sussman, let me ask you this. Do you believe that when the Federal Government establishes new requirements, standards, and mandates, should the Federal Government provide the funds to those local and State jurisdictions to carry them out? Or do you believe that we should continue unfunded Federal mandates?

Mr. SUSSMAN. I think that is a complicated and difficult question, Senator. We need to consider the financial capability of the Federal Government as well as the financial capability of the States.

Senator KEMPTHORNE. What if both are strapped?

Mr. SUSSMAN. Well, if both are strapped, we need to be realistic about our resources, but we also need to keep in mind our environmental goals. We need to find the best way of achieving those goals in a world of limited resources.

Senator KEMPTHORNE. Let me move to another area. As you know from our conversation that we had before, I have some concerns about reregistration for pesticides for minor crops. This is something that I think many, many agricultural States are facing. In the State of Idaho, for example, which is famous for potatoes, interestingly enough, potatoes are considered a minor crop. Because of the burdensome nature of the process of reregistration, many of the manufacturers are questioning if in fact they should continue to manufacture them.

The alternative chemicals are not nearly as effective; in fact, you often have to use larger quantities to p      the crops.

What steps do you think we should be taking at EPA to help in this process of minor crop reregistration?

Mr. SUSSMAN. This is a complicated issue. My understanding is that some pesticide manufacturers are deciding that it's not economical for them to generate the data necessary to support certain minor crop uses, which may be important to farmers but may not be a significant source of revenue for the producers. So they are allowing those applications to be cancelled, which often puts the farmers in a difficult position.

I'm not sure what the answer to this problem is. I do feel that we need to consider not only the interest of the farmers, but the need for adequate, high-quality data to assure the safety of the pesticides. I would hope to be able to dig into this issue more deeply and see if I could evaluate how these interests could best be reconciled.

Senator KEMPTHORNE. So you would help resolve that?

Mr. SUSSMAN. I would hope so.

Senator KEMPTHORNE. All right, thank you very much.

Senator BAUCUS. I note that the ranking member of our committee has just arrived, Senator Chafee.

## OPENING STATEMENT OF HON. JOHN H. CHAFEE, U.S. SENATOR FROM THE STATE OF RHODE ISLAND

Senator CHAFEE. Thank you very much, Mr. Chairman. First of all, I have a statement, and I will put that in the record.

[Senator Chafee's statement follows:]

OPENING STATEMENT OF HON. JOHN H. CHAFEE, U.S. SENATOR FROM THE STATE OF RHODE ISLAND

Thank you, Mr. Chairman, for expeditiously scheduling this hearing to consider the confirmation of Robert M. Sussman to be the Deputy Administrator of the Environmental Protection Agency. It is important that we get high caliber senior managers confirmed and in their jobs as quickly as possible, so that the EPA can get on with the urgent business of protecting this country's environment.

The job of the EPA Deputy Administrator may be one of the more difficult and challenging positions in government. The deputy has traditionally been responsible for overseeing the conduct of nine assistant administrators, and ten far-flung regions, many of whom have their own, oftentimes competing agendas. Bringing cohesion and order to this process requires a manager who can crack the whip when necessary. Mr. Sussman will certainly have his work cut out for him.

Mr. Sussman has an impressive résumé, with considerable expertise in the area of the Toxic Substances Control Act. I have a strong feeling that, if confirmed, he will also become very well acquainted with other statutes, notably the Clean Water Act and CERCLA, and our Superfund law.

Senator CHAFEE. I had an opportunity to meet with Mr. Sussman an we had a very nice talk. I hope that we can move along with this quickly.

Do you have any idea when the other Assistant Administrators will be coming along?

Mr. SUSSMAN. I don't, sorry.

Senator CHAFEE. Well, let's hope it isn't too long, because it is obviously hard for us on this committee to get a gauge of what the Administration is about to do, whether it's the views on clean water or whatever, until there are people in place over there. So I hope Ms. Browner and the White House would clear those folks quickly so that we could get going.

Senator BAUCUS. Thank you.

Senator Faircloth.

Senator FAIRCLOTH. Thank you, Mr. Chairman.

Mr. Sussman, I ran for the Senate pretty much on one program; that is to reduce Federal spending, and no new taxes.

When you start talking about Federal spending and Federal waste—and I know you haven't been confirmed yet, but you have been looking at it for three or four weeks, so I'm not asking you for definitive answers, just in general how you feel.

EPA has a large employment in Raleigh, in the Research Triangle Park area. It has come to my attention that EPA pays the fee for the employees to join a spa, an initial fee of close to $100, then they p      a major portion of the monthly fee for the employees of EPA to be members of a spa.

I'm sure that someone will say, "Well, that's minor money in Government terms." It might be minor money in Government terms, but it's not minor in terms of the working people of this country. It costs the Federal Government a considerable amount of money.

Would you say this is the type of program that is good and should be continued, or should be discontinued? Or you can say, "I haven't had time to study it."

Mr. SUSSMAN. Senator Faircloth, let me respond this way. Good management of the agency is very important to the Administrator and will be very important to me. We want to maximize the benefits of our resources and the productivity of our workforce.

On the issue that you raise, frankly, I haven't had a chance to look into this. I want to get the facts myself firsthand and see what the situation is. I certainly appreciate having it called to my attention.

Senator FAIRCLOTH. So what you're saying is that your general belief is that paying for them to belong to a spa makes them better workers?

Mr. SUSSMAN. No, I'm not saying that at all. I want to make it clear that this is not a situation where I have had an opportunity to investigate. I do want to stress that waste of EPA's resources or EPA's funds is certainly not something that I would condone, and this is a situation that I will look into.

Senator FAIRCLOTH. I just didn't know—I'm 65 years old and have never been inside a spa. In fact, I was 60 before I ever heard what one was. [Laughter.]

But I just wanted to know; if it would make me work better, I might try one. [Laughter.]

One of the EPA's largest concentrations of activity outside of Washington is in Research Triangle Park. The budget in the State is some $350 million; 3,100 people work there. And in a State such as North Carolina, we need all the help we can get, and that payroll certainly means a lot to the State. So nothing I am saying is inclined to mean that we don't want it.

But they have already laid out plans that are well under way for a 625,000-square-foot facility. The first estimate is $260 million, and that will never come in at less than $300 million. You can't even think of less than that.

They are currently paying $15 million a year in rent, but they want to build this new facility. Figuring it any way you want to, 7 percent interest on $300 million is $21 million in just interest alone on the new facility, not counting any of the other things that come with it.

Do you think this is a good expenditure of Federal Government money, when we're going in debt at over $1 billion a day now, when the taxpayers of this country are severely strapped and have clearly indicated they don't want any more taxes? And what they want is reduced spending? Do you think it's wise to be going on with a $300 million building, which I understand is to include a lot of amenities that are not normally available in the average commercial building?

Just a yes or no on that.

Mr. SUSSMAN. Well, let me try to steer in between the yes and the no——

Senator FAIRCLOTH. No, you don't need to steer between them. Do you think it's a good expenditure of money?

Mr. SUSSMAN. I don't know enough about it to make a judgment.

Senator FAIRCLOTH. All right, that's a good answer. That's a good one.

The budget has gone up consistently. We talk about reducing the budget, reducing spending. I have been in the Senate for what soon will be four months, and I had always thought reduced spending and reducing the budget meant spending less money. I had never understood it meant slowing down the rate at which you intended to increase, that that was reducing spending.

But anyway, the EPA budget has gone from $4.9 billion to $5.9 billion from 1988 to 1992. Inflation was 16 percent, but it was a 20 percent increase in the EPA budget. Now the President has proposed a budget that goes from $5.9 billion in 1992 to $7 billion in 1996, an 18 percent increase. Of course, he has projected inflation at 11 percent in that time, or a 7 percent increase in EPA's budget over the expected or past rate of inflation.

We're talking about sacrifices. In fact, the President has used that word a number of times. His State of the Union speech said that the public had to make sacrifices; that we no longer pay taxes, we are making contributions as a sacrifice to the Government.

Do you not feel—and this would take a yes or no answer—that it is time that the Federal Government itself, including EPA, made some sacrifices?

Mr. SUSSMAN. I think that the entire Federal Government needs to manage its resources very carefully and prudently. And yes, there is a duty to make sacrifices. But I do want to point out that my understanding is that prior to 1988, EPA's budget was flat for an extended period, while the Congress was adding to the agency's responsibilities. I do feel that we need to keep in mind the large volume of work that the agency is required to do, and certainly within that context to look for economies and sacrifices wherever we can justify them.

Senator BAUCUS. Thank you very much, Senator.

I think Mr. Sussman actually makes a good point. I've forgotten the exact figures, but it's my recollection that during the 1980's the EPA budget was not only flat, but it was substantially cut.

Senator FAIRCLOTH. In terms of money?

Senator BAUCUS. Dollars. And it raises some very fundamental questions. What is the proper level of resources that an agency should have?

I know in many respects some of the problems that the States have had with EPA result from cutbacks in EPA resources in certain areas. It is hard for EPA to develop the technical guidelines and the standards when the resources are being cut back.

This is not an EPA example, but take grazing fees as an example. One basic reason why BLM does not adequately oversee grazing allotments on BLM lands is because they don't have the personnel, don't have the resources. BLM estimates that about 50 percent of grazing allotments on public lands, on BLM lands, is just not monitored because there are no resources. BLM does not have the resources.

It's just a basic question that we have to ask. Cutting Government makes good sense, but frankly, there are other goals. What we really want is efficient Government. I think that is the proper goal, rather than just cutting Government for the sake of cutting Government. I know the Senator agrees with that statement, but there are no easy answers to these questions. But I appreciate the thrust of the Senator's question.

Senator FAIRCLOTH. Mr. Chairman, does the land that the BLM rents for grazing fees not bring in enough money to pay for supervision of the grazing?

Senator BAUCUS. Well, that would not be sufficient.

Senator FAIRCLOTH. The income from the grazing fees does not bring in enough money to supervise the land?

Senator BAUCUS. First of all, we need reform in BLM grazing. There's no doubt about that. In fact, Secretary of the Interior Babbitt is going out west to hold a series of four hearings—this is not an EPA matter—a series of four hearings throughout the west on grazing fees and what should be the proper level of grazing fees. I believe that grazing fees should be increased. The question is, what is the proper level?

In addition to increasing grazing fees, if we're honest about all this, we need a better approach to monitoring leases to be sure that they're not overgrazed, to be sure that cattle aren't bunching up, for example, too close to streams in certain cases. It takes a conservation plan and you need investment, whether it's stock ponds or fencing or other investments to make sure that the land is properly managed. Sometimes that takes a few dollars. And the fact is that there's a major difference between private grazing and public grazing, because in public grazing you're farther away from roads because you're further up the mountains, you have a greater distance to travel, and stockmen have to build fences, which is not the case with private leases; and developing water, for example, which is not the case with private leases.

First, there should be reform. Second, fees can and should be increased. And third, you need a more comprehensive way of managing this, which probably does include some resources, so that the BLM knows whether or not the allotments are properly managed. It's a resource question and it's an efficiency question.

Senator CHAFEE. May I ask one question?

Senator BAUCUS. Yes, sir.

Senator CHAFEE. My knowledge of grazing fees is extremely limited, so I won't get into that, but I suspect, in answer to the distinguished Senator's question, that the grazing fees probably go into the General Treasury——

Senator BAUCUS. They do.

Senator CHAFEE [continuing]. And are not held by the BLM to supervise the allotments.

What I wanted to say, though, is that you're right, the budget of the EPA has gone up. One of the reasons, as Mr. Sussman said, is that we cheerfully add new responsibilities. For example, just a couple of years ago we passed legislation dealing with the supervision of medical waste. We were finding syringes washed up on the beaches of Long Island, and so forth. So everybody got outraged, and zingo, we passed a bill that provided that there shall be supervision of the disposal of medical waste.

Who does it? EPA. I have a list here, the Indoor Radon Abatement Act of 1988; the Ocean Dumping Act of 1988; Hazardous and

Solid Waste Amendments of 1984; the Clean Water Act of 1987; and, of course, the Clean Air Act that we passed in 1990. All of these levy tremendous new responsibility on EPA. That doesn't mean that their budget can't be carefully watched, and the question is a good one.

Senator BAUCUS. Yes.

For the record, this is EPA's spending level for roughly the last 13 years. In 1980, the EPA budget was $5.6 billion in spending. In 1984, four years later, it was cut to $4.1 billion. That's more than a 25 percent reduction. In 1988, though, it went up to $4.9 billion, which is about an 18 percent increase. And then in 1992, $5.9 billion. So from $5.6 billion in 1980, it is $5.9 billion in 1992. So it has essentially been up and down.

Senator FAIRCLOTH. Mr. Chairman, if I may, to both the distinguished Senators, I absolutely understand the problems. But yet, if there is a Federal agency that isn't in the same situation, asking for more money—the Defense Department, I think, has agreed that some cuts are going to be made there—but with the exception of the Defense Department, is there an agency that has agreed that they've got to be cut and can be cut in real dollars?

Senator BAUCUS. I agree with the Senator. I do not know of an agency that wants fewer dollars. Everybody wants more dollars. But that's our responsibility, in working with the President, to find that right allocation.

I would like to turn it back over to the nominee, though.

Mr. Sussman, in your view, what is working at EPA? What are its best attributes? What does not need to be fixed, as you understand it?

Mr. SUSSMAN. Well, EPA has a strong and motivated workforce, as I indicated, which I believe over the years has done an exceptionally good job in responding to the vagaries and stresses that have been placed on EPA.

Senator BAUCUS. So you think the workforce is pretty good?

Mr. SUSSMAN. I think the workforce is pretty good. I think the framework for many of EPA's programs is basically sound.

Senator BAUCUS. Okay. Now, what's the biggest problem facing the agency, as you see it?

Mr. SUSSMAN. As I see it, the biggest problem is the need to create a vision of environmental protection which moves beyond the end-of-pipe focus of many of the statutes that EPA implements. Those statutes are important; the mandates they impose are critical. Those mandates have to be met, but the public needs to perceive EPA as more than a collection of fiefdoms dedicated to the Clean Water Act, Clean Air Act, RCRA, FIFRA, etc. There needs to be a larger vision of environmental protection which the public can understand and relate to.

I think some of the themes that Administrator Browner has articulated will move us toward that larger vision.

Senator BAUCUS. I appreciate that, but let me tell you that it's my impression that both you and the Administrator—because you're the top people—are going to have to grab this agency, get hold of it, and begin to reform it in many areas. One is the contracting practice of the agency; because it does not have personnel in many cases, it contracts out even the job of developing regulations. It has become a mess, frankly. Consequently many people in our country, whether they be farmers or ranchers or businesspeople or the State regulators, often just throw their hands up in disgust at red tape, at bureaucracy, at perceived insensitivity of the EPA.

I think EPA has done a great job in many areas, but I also have to tell you that I think one of your major challenges and one of your major goals should be just to get hold of the agency, to shape it up, and to be sure that your people are "people-sensitive" to the people they're regulating. You have a long way to go, because the image of EPA in many parts of this country is not good.

I have to tell you that in talking to members of the Senate on matters dealing with EPA, I run into a large groundswell of problems facing the EPA. I think that essentially the Senators are reflecting what they hear from home.

Again, EPA has done a great job in many areas. Frankly, it is my goal—as it is your goal—to help make this a better agency, but I have to tell you that you're thepone there that can get the job done or not get the job done. You have an immense task ahead of you. It gets at a more user-friendly apparatus, sending people out under a multidisciplinary approach under the Clean Water Act and Clean Air Act and so forth, so that a company knows that when it is dealing with the EPA, it is kind of a one-stop process. In many cases a company doesn't know which agency to go to, which part of which agency to go to, because the different statutes have different programs and different people administering those different programs. Many companies just pull their hair out as a consequence. Theseyare well-meaning businesspeople. They're not trying to avoid the law; they're just trying to get the job done.

I am sure there are some who do try to avoid the law, and you should prosecute those people vigorously. But I'm talking about the people not trying to avoid the law, and there are many of them, who are just overburdened with excessive red tape and bureaucracy and insensitivity.

I also strongly urge you to get your people out of Washington more, out of the regional offices, out to where the people are. I would guess that there may be too many mid-level management people in EPA. I don't know that, but that would just be an operating assumption of mine. It's not necessarily that you want to cut the number of personnel; it's rather that you want to get the personnel out in the field, talking to people, putting themselves in the shoes of real, ordinary people, finding out what their problems really are. Most Americans want to do the right thing; by far, most Americans do. They don't want to break the law; they just don't want to get hassled unnecessarily and just beat upon unnecessarily.

I don't want to overstate this point, and it sounds kind of corny, but we're all public servants. We work for those people. They are our employers. They are our bosses. Often the attitude at Federal agencies is just the reverse, that somehow they are above people, they dictate to people. Usually, in an employer-employee relationship, it's the employers that say what they want, not the employees who dictate. I don't want to carry the analogy too far here, but I just think you have a fundamental task ahead of you. I very much hope you understand it, because if you do, at theyend of your tenure at the new department, you're going to feel that you've really accomplished something. If you don't, you may leave in great frustration.

Mr. SUSSMAN. Let me say that I take these points very much to heart. I take them very seriously. I do understand the challenge ahead of me, and I will keep your thoughts very much in mind.

Senator BAUCUS. And you're going to have to have the zeal and the laser-like focus and dedication almost of a junkyard dog to get this done. It is going to take tremendous energy and focus, and you have our cooperation.

Senator Chafee.

Senator CHAFEE. Thank you.

I want to point out to Senator Faircloth that he's onto something when he is worrying about whether any agency ever goes down in its budget. I refer you to Parkinson, who wrote a book about Parkinson's Law, dealing with Great Britain. He pointed out that there are more employees in the British Naval Office, with the remnants of a tiny fleet, than there were when the British Fleet was at its peak. He also noted that the British Colonial Office has more employees than when Britain had a vast empire.

So based on that, I did some research with the ICC, the Interstate Commerce Commission to see, when we deregulated all trucking, whether the number of employees in the ICC, where you used to have to go to get permission to have a route, and you were supervised—whether the number of employees in the ICC did decline. I thought you could abolish the ICC, but that's too traumatic to occur in the Government.

But indeed, I did find that the number of employees in the ICC did decline after we deregulated. If I check now, maybe it's crept back up again to its original heights, for all I know. But be of good cheer; sometimes the number of employees does decline.

I would just like to say this, Mr. Sussman. One of the problems with which I am concerned with is industrial sites within a city that have become contaminated, probably not qualifying for a Superfund listing, and thus no other employer or manufacturer or builder or whoever will go into these sites because of the potential liability under the Superfund program.

So you've got a contradiction here. I have a specific instance in our capital city, Providence, but it extends across the Nation, where you want to get employers to come into the city, but they won't go near the place because of the potential liability. Thus they go out and do exactly what we don't want them to do; they go out in the country and take over some lovely potato field and pave it and build their plant there, and we've lost all the way around. The inner city employees can't get there. We don't have the tax base for the cities. We have to construct new sewage treatment and new water facilities for this plant out in the country.

I don't have a solution, but I'm just asking you to put it down on your "worry list" and give it some thought. What we would like, obviously, is—why don't the cities clean them up? Well, they can't afford to. Now, can you tap the Superfund program for it? They're not listed on the Priority List. Do you have any thoughts on that? I'm not expecting you to come up with an immediate solution.

Mr. SUSSMAN. This is a serious problem, and it's a particularly serious problem at our older eastern cities which have experienced significant industrialization early in the century.

I don't know what the answer is. I know there are proposals pending to create incentives for voluntary cleanup, perhaps by eliminating residual liability for those who step up to the mark and do a voluntary cleanup in a situation where the Superfund program doesn't apply. Perhaps that's an answer that needs to be looked at.

I recognize this is a serious problem and I will try to take a look at it, if I am confirmed.

Senator CHAFEE. OK. Well, thank you. That's all I can ask. Maybe somehow we can change the liability situation, because nobody wants to get into it; once they start into this mess, then they become liable for the whole thing, and they don't want to touch it.

Thank you, Mr. Chairman.

Senator BAUCUS. Thank you.

Senator Kempthorne.

Senator KEMPTHORNE. Mr. Sussman, I would make a suggestion, and that is that the chairman's comments about the red tape, about how the average citizen is being impacted, the fact that we are all public servants, is something that you ought to make a copy of, and throughout your tenure glance at it once in a while. I think it's a good reminder to all of us.

You stated in your comments, "Minority and low income communities should not be subject disproportionately to environmental hazards, nor should they suffer from neglect by Federal environmental officials."

The flip side to that is that there are a number of communities that you may consider low income communities, but it's not neglect from Federal officials that is of concern to them. It's the fact of the regulations that are brought with those Federal officials, and an attitude not of "How can we help you to achieve these standards," but, "Until you achieve these standards, you will be fined $25,000 a day."

That's not a solution to a low income community. So we need that cooperation. I would stress that.

Let me ask you this. There is a school of thought that recognition and improved enforcement of private property rights is essential to genuine environmental protection. This school attributes the abandonment of this principle and its associated common law by the courts during the industrial revolution as a precursor to the environmental degradation that later followed.

What are your views on the relationship between private property and environmental protection?

Mr. SUSSMAN. That's a very complicated area.

We do have guarantees in our Constitution against the taking of property without just compensation. Those are important guarantees. There are judicial remedies available to enforce them.

I think the question is whether we need to go beyond the Constitutional protections and build some additional protections into our statues and regulations. That's a difficult issue. I don't know the answer to that. I think we have to avoid hobbling our Environmental Protection Agency with additional requirements that make it more difficult for them to do their jobs. On the other hand, the protection of property rights is important, and we need to take that into account. This is an area that I would hope to learn more about.

Senator KEMPTHORNE. Let me take it from a different direction, then. Under a current Executive Order, EPA is required, in certain of its regulatory and other actions, to analyze whether, and to what extent, its action will constitute a taking of private property rights under the 5th Amendment.

The Senate has already voted twice to codify the Executive Order. In fact, it is likely to do so again today. I understand EPA has been somewhat slow in undertaking that analysis, and in fact, it fought inside the White House to oppose the Bush Administration's endorsement of codification.

Since the courts are beginning to acknowledge that regulatory actions can be of the magnitude as to become a taking, resulting in judgments against the Federal Government in millions of dollars, will you take steps to assure compliance with that Executive Order?

Mr. SUSSMAN. I have not had a chance to review the Executive Order in detail. I can't speak to the steps that the EPA has to take to assure compliance.

As I indicated, I would like to become more knowledgeable about the takings issue, because I think it raises complex issues. I would certainly want to look at the Executive Order and find out more about what steps EPA is or is not taking to comply.

Senator KEMPTHORNE. Do you consider yourself an advocate of private property rights?

Mr. SUSSMAN. I consider myself a defender of the Constitution. [Laughter.]

Senator CHAFEE. I think it would be very unusual to have somebody come before us who said, "I don't consider myself a defender of the Constitution." [Laughter.]

You haven't made much news by being for the Constitution. [Laughter.]

Senator KEMPTHORNE. Are you a strong advocate for private property rights?

Mr. SUSSMAN. I certainly do believe in private property rights.

Senator KEMPTHORNE. Do you still want the job? [Laughter.]

Mr. SUSSMAN. I think I do.

Senator KEMPTHORNE. Thank you, Mr. Chairman.

Senator BAUCUS. Thank you.

Mr. Sussman, just a couple of points I would like you to think about and pursue as Deputy Administrator. I will address two separate areas.

One is hearings on environmental technologies. You mentioned this in your statement, and I would just like to underline it for you, about the need for this country to bridge the gap between economic development and environmental protection—to pursue environmental technologies, not only end-of-the-pipe technologies, but as you mentioned in your statement pollution prevention, life cycle planning, etc., and in many respects, pursuing the goal of sustainable development. Obviously, we cannot have a strong economy without a healthy environment and without strong environmental protection, and we can't have strong environmental protection without a healthy economy. As you said, they go hand-in-hand.

This is one way to end the religious wars that generally occur between economic interests on the one hand and environmentalists and the conservation community on the other. It's an area where I think there is common ground, and I very, very much urge you, in the rules and regulations and in implementing the statutes that we authorize, to work to pursue that goal.

I say so for a lot of reasons. The basic reason is because it's the only option we have. It's the one that makes the most sense. Second, other countries are very aggressively pursuing this approach. They are developing environmental technologies and they are selling them worldwide. Senator Chafee and I were both at the Earth Summit down at Rio de Janeiro and learned there how the Japanese are peddling their environmental technologies, and the Germans are, too, and we Americans are just not doing a very good job of doing that.

Now, it's a very large, emerging market. It's a $200 billion market worldwide, growing at 10 percent a year. The growth potential is unlimited in developing environmental technologies. It is obvious that as other parts of the world find their economies growing and growth rates increasing, that there is going to be greater demand for environmental protection.

Just anecdotally, I was talking to a fellow with a big worldwide shipping firm who said that they are now finding that it is hard for them to locate families in some Southeast Asian countries because the water is not safe to drink anymore, and the other environmental problems they are facing. This is a new development for this shipping firm; it only occurred recently. I would suspect that at least in Southeast Asia, where the economies are growing by leaps and bounds, as you know—the growth rate in China last year was 13 percent, annual growth rate of 13 percent. Many of us have been to these countries, to Hong Kong and southern China, and it's amazing how quickly these economies are growing. And they're going to demand greater environmental protection.

As you also know, in the European Community, they have takeback provisions for recycling and pollution prevention that are very stringent. Most Americans think we couldn't begin to abide by those standards, but obviously if we gave a little thought to it and developed environmental technologies, we could do it pretty well.

So I urge you very strongly to pursue work in this area, because I think it is the future in environmental protection generally, generically, in this country.

The second area really gets at developing a much better environmental database and coordinating all the various environmental data that are available, so that there is a better connection, a nexus between environmental degradation on one hand and remedies on the other. One example of where there is some strain here is Superfund. Superfund is very expensive, and it's obvious that we have to clean up these sites; that's clear. But perhaps with better data, better focussed, we might find other remedies which solve the problem, which address the environmental degradation but perhaps are less expensive.

I urge you, too, to work on that database and look at how to get the right data and ask the right questions and coordinate the various databases that States and private entities have.

On that point, as you know, a lot of companies have databases, but EPA just doesn't utilize them very well, probably because there is not sufficient trust between the two. I urge you to look for ways to go to companies, not with a view to slapping some citations on them for failure to live up to certain environmental statutes and standards, but rather to work with the company to try to work up a plan to resolve the problems in a nonadversarial, because then you're going to get the cooperation of the company. They want to solve these problems, too; they just don't want to be hassled by the EPA. Obviously, if a company does not want to resolve it, you'll find that out pretty quickly and you can take appropriate remedial action.

But these are areas which, if pursued aggressively, will go a long way toward solving the perception that a lot of people in this country have, that EPA just kind of rides roughshod over them, that it is insensitive, and so forth.

I'm not saying that we ought to lessen environmental protection. On the contrary, I'm saying we want to enhance it and improve upon it and have greater environmental protection in this country, but in a way that is less threatening, that is more sensitive, that is more effective. The real target here is effectiveness. We want to be effective. Sometimes effectiveness takes a little bit of creativity and a little extra work to be effective, and I just urge you to do that.

Mr. SUSSMAN. I will keep that in mind.

Senator BAUCUS. Okay.

I have no further questions, Mr. Sussman. We will take your nomination under advisement at a very near date. The committee will meet and act upon your nomination. We cannot today at this moment do so, but we will do so at an early date.

Mr. SUSSMAN. I appreciate it very much, Mr. Chairman.

Senator BAUCUS. Thank you.

The hearing is adjourned.

[Whereupon, at 10:45 a.m., the committee adjourned, to reconvene at the call of the Chair.]

[Mr. Sussman's p statement and responses to a Committee questionnaire follow:]

### STATEMENT OF ROBERT M. SUSSMAN
### NOMINATED TO BE DEPUTY ADMINISTRATOR
### U.S. ENVIRONMENTAL PROTECTION AGENCY

### APRIL 28, 1993

Mr. Chairman and Members of the Committee:

On behalf of myself and the Administrator, I want to thank the Committee for the opportunity to appear at this hearing and for the opportunity to meet informally with many members of the Committee and the staff over the last two weeks. These meetings provided me with an invaluable understanding of the agenda of the Committee and will help me immensely in performing my responsibilities if I am confirmed.

I am very honored that the President and Administrator have asked me to serve as EPA Deputy Administrator. This is a challenging and demanding job but one that offers great rewards. This Administration is committed to a new vision of environmental protection that will change the relationship between our citizens and the world around us. As the President has observed frequently, economic growth and strong environmental safeguards are not incompatible but mutually reinforcing. I share this vision fully and, if confirmed, will do all I can to help the Administrator and the President to make it a reality.

-2-

Before discussing the issues facing EPA, I wanted to share with the Committee a few observations about my background and experience.

I was born in New York City shortly after the end of World War II and have always considered New York my home. I went to college and law school in the late 1960s and early 1970s and was shaped by the idealism of that turbulent but hopeful period in our history.

After eight years at Yale University, I became a practicing lawyer in Washington in 1974. My practice has primarily involved health, safety and environmental issues, although I have devoted considerable time to pro bono work. While my clients have been drawn from the private sector, I have worked extensively with environmental groups, EPA and other agencies. I have developed great respect for the environmental community, whose leadership and determination have helped to forge many of the successful environmental programs that are in place today. I have also developed great respect for the EPA career staff, whose extraordinary professionalism, expertise and capacity for hard work have sustained the Agency during its difficult periods and made possible the Agency's numerous accomplishments. I look forward to joining them in serving our country and protecting our environment.

Based on my years of practice, I feel I have developed valuable skills that can help the Agency. They include not only extensive knowledge of environmental science and policy, but patience, a willingness to listen to the concerns of EPA's many stakeholders, and a strong commitment to consensus-building. I take considerable pride in the key role I played in negotiated rulemaking when I was in private practice. I hope to use this experience to help the Administrator fulfill her goal of building new partnerships between EPA, State and local governments, industry and the environmental community.

Although consensus and dialogue are essential for effective decisionmaking, it is ultimately EPA's responsibility to set our environmental goals and decide how to meet them. Strong leadership in performing these functions is absolutely critical. While EPA should listen to the views of its stakeholders, the Agency has an obligation to make clear policy choices which are communicated to the regulated community in a timely and understandable manner. Standards and regulations implementing these policies should then be enforced fairly but vigorously. In my work with industry, I have observed first-hand the value of ambitious, technology-forcing standards which challenge our companies to make the investments we need for long-term environmental improvement and economic strength. I am convinced that if EPA exercises strong leadership, American industry will cooperate with the Agency and use its considerable talents to meet and surpass EPA's environmental goals without any loss of competitiveness.

EPA's leadership role will be tested in the years ahead as we tackle the many unfinished portions of our environmental agenda. The Administrator has identified several ambitious goals for the Agency and, if I am confirmed, it will be my role to help her achieve them. I would like to highlight some of these goals in order to illustrate the areas where I hope to make a contribution to the Agency:

- Pollution prevention should be a cornerstone of all of EPA's programs so that our industries have every incentive to use waste minimization and new manufacturing processes to prevent the creation of pollution at the source. Pollution prevention will lessen our reliance on end-of-pipe controls which are often ineffective and will help stimulate the technological innovation that we need for economic growth.

- Ecosystem protection (or the protection of entire natural systems) should become a goal of EPA's programs equal in importance to the protection of human health. This means a new sensitivity to ecological concerns in EPA's decisionmaking and a new emphasis on geographical initiatives and other cross-

-5-

media programs which focus on the interrelationships between different species and the control of multiple pollution sources in achieving environmental quality.

● EPA should continue to improve the science base it uses for decisionmaking. This involves not only strengthening the quality of the data which EPA relies on but assuring that the Agency seeks the most knowledgeable experts inside and outside the Agency when it tackles complex and important scientific issues.

● EPA should build new partnerships with State and local governments which strengthen our environmental infrastructure, streamline decisionmaking and use federal resources to better support State programs.

● Environmental justice should be a guiding principle for decisionmaking at EPA. Minority and low-income communities should not be subject disproportionately to environmental hazards, nor should they suffer from neglect by federal environmental officials.

-6-

As you know, the Administrator is committed to tackling not just these but other critical environmental issues facing our nation. If confirmed, it will be an honor to assist her in any way I can. I will also make every effort to build a productive and cooperative relationship with the Congress and with this Committee.

Thank you very much and I will be pleased to answer your questions.

UNITED STATES SENATE

COMMITTEE ON ENVIRONMENT AND PUBLIC WORKS

STATEMENT FOR COMPLETION BY PRESIDENTIAL NOMINEES

Name _____ SUSSMAN _____ ROBERT _____ MATTHEW _____
          (Last)                (First)          (Middle)

Position to        DEPUTY ADMINISTRATOR            Date of
which nominated: ENVIRONMENTAL PROTECTION AGENCY   Nomination: ____ MARCH 17, 1993

Date of birth ____ 12/8/47 _____ Place of birth ___ Brooklyn, New York _____
              (Day) (Month) (Year)

Marital status: ___ Married _____ Full name of spouse: __ Judith Hidden Lanius ____

Name and ages
of children    Benjamin Lanius Sussman                    2 years 4 months

Education

| Institution | Dates attended | Degrees received | Dates of degrees |
|---|---|---|---|
| Garden City High School/NY | 1961-65 | Diploma | 6/65 |
| Yale College/New Haven, CT | 1965-69 | B.A. | 6/69 |
| Yale Graduate School | 1969-70 | --- | --- |
| Yale Law School | 1970-73 | LLD | 6/73 |

Employment      List all positions held since college, including the title and description of job, name
record          of employer, location, and dates. If you were terminated involuntarily from any
                position(s), please note the circumstances
                1- New York Urban Coalition, New York City - Intern - Preparing Reports
                   on Urban Problems - Summer 1969
                2- Brooklyn District Attorney's Office, Brooklyn, NY - Legal Intern - Doing
                   Legal Research and Investigation - Summer 1971
                3- U.S. Army Reserve/Connecticut National Guard (served in New Haven, CT;
                   Boston, MA; Philadelphia,PA and Rockville, MD) - specialized in
                   administration and communications - 1970-76
                4- Covington and Burling, Washington, DC - Summer Associate - Did legal
                   research - Summer 1972
                5- Clerk, Hon. Walter K. Stapleton (US District Court for Delaware) -
                   performed legal research - 6/73-6/74

Employment record—Continued

6- Covington and Burling, Washington, DC - Associate Attorney - (6/74-9/81); ~~Partner (9/81-10/87)~~

7- Latham & Watkins, Washington, DC - Partner (10/87-3/93)

| | |
|---|---|
| Honors and awards. | List significant scholarships, fellowships, honorary degrees, military medals, honorary society memberships, and any other special recognitions for outstanding service or achievement. |

Phi Beta Kappa (Yale College)

Magna Cum Laude (Yale College)

Snow Prize for Outstanding Essay on American Literature (Yale College)

Wrexham Prize for Outstanding Essay in Humanities (Yale College)

Carnegie Fellowship(Yale University)
Editor, Yale Law Journal (Yale Law School)

Finalist, Moot Court Competition (Yale Law School)

| | |
|---|---|
| Memberships | List significant memberships and offices held in professional, fraternal, business, scholarly, civic, charitable and other organizations |

| Organization | Office held (if any) | Dates |
|---|---|---|
| District of Columbia Bar | Admin. Law Steering Comm. | Early 1980's |
| American Civil Liberties Union | ———— | 1980's-Present |
| Manuscript Society (at Yale Univ) | ———— | 1980's-Present |
| Environmental Law Institute | ———— | 1988-Present |
| Georgetown Citizens Association | ———— | 1989-Present |

**Qualifications:** State fully your qualifications to serve in the position to which you have been named My career as a practicing attorney and student of the regulatory process spans nearly 20 years. As a result of this experience, I have obtained broad familiarity with EPA as an institution and with the nation's environmental laws and regulations. I have also developed a working knowledge of the scientific disciplines that affect environmental policy. Working with the Agency, environmental groups and industry, I have come to appreciate the importance our society attaches to enhanced environmental quality as well as the value of consensus and dialogue in achieving our shared environmental goals. I strongly support the commitment of the President and the Administrator to combining economic growth with strong environmental protection.

**Future employment relationships:**

1. Indicate whether you will sever all connections with your present employer, business firm, association or organization if you are confirmed by the Senate
I have already severed these connections.

2. As far as can be foreseen, state whether you have any plans after completing government service to resume employment, affiliation or practice with your current or any previous employer, business firm, association or organization
I have no such plans at this time.

3. Has anybody made a commitment to you for a job after you leave government?
NO

4. (a) If you have been appointed for a fixed term, do you expect to serve the full term?
N/A

(b) If you have been appointed for an indefinite term, do you have any known limitations on your willingness or ability to serve for the foreseeable future?

NO

(c) If you have previously held any Schedule C or other appointive position in the Executive branch, irrespective of whether the position required Congressional confirmation, please state the circumstances of your departure and its timing

NO

**Financial Statement.**

1  Attach a copy of your Executive Personnel Financial Disclosure Report (SF 278)

2  List sources, amounts and dates of all anticipated receipts from deferred income arrangements, stock options, uncompleted contracts and other future benefits which you expect to derive from previous business relationships, professional services and firm memberships or from former employers, clients, and customers. Amounts should be indicated by the categories established for reporting income on Form SF 278, Schedule A.

The only deferred income and other arrangements I have with my

former firm involve continued participation in its retirement plan

($110,000) and medical plan.

3. Are any assets pledged? (Add schedule)

NO

4. Are you currently a party to any legal action?

NO

5  Have you filed a Federal income tax return for each of the last 10 years? If not, please explain the circumstances.

YES

6 Has the Internal Revenue Service ever audited your Federal tax return? If so, what resulted from the audit?

It is possible an audit was conducted several (over 10) years ago, but

I cannot clearly recollect it and have no documentation.

Potential conflicts of interest

1 Describe any financial or deferred compensation agreements or other continuing dealings with business associates, clients or customers who will be affected by policies which you will influence in the position to which you have been nominated

NONE

2 List any investments, obligations, liabilities, or other relationships which might involve potential conflicts of interest, or the appearance of conflicts of interest, with the position to which you have been nominated

These issues have been discussed with EPA's Ethics Officer and are

addressed in my recusal statement, which has been issued to certain

EPA employees and will be reissued following my confirmation.

3 Describe any business relationship, dealing or financial transaction (other than taxpaying) which you have had during the last 10 years with the Federal Government, whether for yourself or relatives, on behalf of a client, or acting as an agent, that might in any way constitute or result in a possible conflict of interest, or an appearance of conflict of interest, with the position to which you have been nominated

NONE

4 Explain how you will resolve any potential conflict of interest, or appearance of a conflict of interest, that may be disclosed by your responses to the above items

My ethics agreement with EPA, which has been provided to the

Committee, should resolve all issues.

5  Explain how you will comply with conflict of interest laws and regulations applicable to the position for which you have been nominated Attach a statement from the
   appropriate agency official indicating what those laws and regulations are and how
   you will comply with them. For this purpose, you may utilize a statement by the
   relevant agency Ethics Officer

I have agreed to various recusals and other restrictions to observe

applicable laws and regulations.  My ethics agreement with EPA explains

the commitments I have made.

---

**Political affiliation and activities**

List all memberships and offices held in, or financial contributions (in excess of
$ 1,000), and services rendered to any political party or election committee during
the last 10 years.

1992 – DNC Victory Fund – $2500 (together with wife)

1992 – Clinton for President – $1500 (together with wife)

In 1988, we made contributions to the Gore for President Committee and

DNC, but do not have records of exact amounts.  We also made

contributions to Gore Senate races.

---

**Published writings:**

List the titles, publishers and dates of any books, articles, or reports you have written
(Please list first any publications and/or speeches that involve environmental or
related matters )

I have delivered several speeches at various seminars relating to

environmental issues.  I cannot identify such speeches at this time.

Publications I have authored are as follows:

(1) Robert M. Sussman and Peter Barton Hutt, Premanufacture Notification in
Guidebook: Toxic Substances Control Act, CRC Press (1981) (G. Dominguez, Ed.)

(2) Herbert Dym & Robert M. Sussman, Antitrust and Electric utility Regulation
XXVIII Antitrust Bulletin 69 (1983)

(3) Robert M. Sussman, John Seymour and Kenneth Ross, Can Private Parties Sue
Under an Interpretative Rule? National Law Journal, V.7, p. 20 (Aug. 19,1985)

(4) Robert M. Sussman, An Overview of the OSHA Hazard Communication Standard
and Key Issues of Interpretation, 42 Food Drug Cosmetic Law Journal 307-314

(5) Robert M. Sussman and Peter L. Winik, The Consumer Product Safety
Improvement Act of 1990, 18 Product  Safety and Liability Reporter 1434-1440

(6) Robert M. Sussman, Julia A. Hatcher and Andrew T. Kreig, Preparing a
Defensible MSDS – Legal Requirements and Liability Considerations in
Material Safety Data Sheets:  Writer's Desk Reference, Hill & Garnett
Publishing (1992)                          6

In addition to the above, I authored an article on exemptions from the new substance review
process under the Toxic Substances Control Act which was published in the Environmental Forum in
the early 1980's.  I also authored an article on reporting requirements under the Consumer
Product Safety Act which was published in the Legal Times of Washington in the mid 1980's.  I have
searched for citations to these articles but have not been able to locate them

_____

_____

_____

_____

**Additional Matters:**

1    If there is any additional information which you believe may be pertinent to the Members of the Committee in reaching their decisions, you may include that here

NO

_____

_____

2    Do you agree to appear before all Congressional Committees which seek your testimony?

YES

3    Having completed this form, are there any additional questions which you believe the Committee should ask of future nominees?

NO

_____

_____

_____

**AFFIDAVIT**

ROBERT M. SUSSMAN

_____) ss, being duly sworn, hereby states that he/she has read and signed the foregoing Statement for Completion by Presidential Nominees including the Financial Statement and that the information provided therein is, to the best of his/her knowledge and belief, current, accurate, and complete.

_Robert M. Sussman_

Subscribed and sworn before me this   2   day of _April_ , 19 93

_Samuel Robinson_
Notary Public

SAMUEL ROBINSON
NOTARY PUBLIC STATE Of MARYLAND
My Commission Expires August 23, 1994

7
O